13140003041000

 # The Library
IN EAST AYRSHIRE

 East Ayrshire
COUNCIL

Please return item by last date shown,
or contact library to renew

Jesus Christ
parables
miracles

D1391510

Education Resource Service

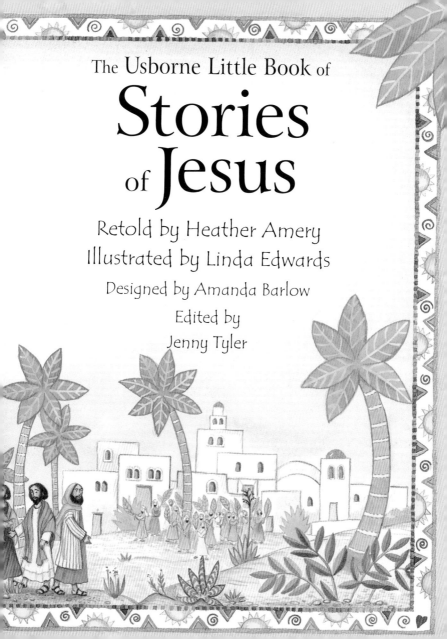

The Usborne Little Book of

Stories
of Jesus

Retold by Heather Amery

Illustrated by Linda Edwards

Designed by Amanda Barlow

Edited by
Jenny Tyler

Contents

Mary and the Angel

Mary lived in Nazareth, a village in the hills of Galilee. She was engaged to be married to Joseph, a carpenter who lived in the village.

One day, God sent an angel called Gabriel to Mary. "Don't be frightened," he said. "God has sent me to tell you that you will have a son and you must call him Jesus. He will be a great King and his kingdom will last forever."

Mary was very puzzled. "I don't understand," she said to Gabriel. "How can I have a son? I'm not married yet."

"It will be the work of God, who can do anything," said Gabriel. "Your son will be holy and will be the Son of God."

Mary bowed her head. "I am God's servant. I'll do what He wants," she said. When she looked up, Gabriel had gone.

Joseph was a kind man but when he heard

that Mary was expecting a baby, he
thought it was not right for him
to marry her.

That night, he had a
dream. In it an angel
told him that he should
marry Mary and that her
son was the Son of God. He
would be called Jesus and he would
save people from God's punishment for the bad things
they had done.

Next day, Joseph remembered what the angel had told
him. He made arrangements for the wedding and soon
they were married. Joseph vowed to take care of Mary
and her baby son.

The Birth of Jesus

Mary and Joseph lived happily together and looked forward to the birth of the baby Mary was expecting. A few months later, the Roman Emperor Augustus, who ruled the whole country, made a new law. Everyone must go to the town their family came from to register so they could be taxed. Joseph's family had come from Bethlehem, so he had to go back there.

He started on the long journey with Mary, who was expecting her baby quite soon. They loaded up their donkey with warm clothes, food, water, and things for the baby.

It was late when they reached Bethlehem and Mary was very tired. The small town was crowded and noisy with all the people who had come to register. Joseph tried to find a room to stay in for the night, but everywhere was already full up. He trudged through the cold, dark streets, leading the donkey Mary rode on.

He knocked on the door of the last inn but it was already

full, not one room left. There was a stable nearby though, which was clean and empty.

Joseph led the donkey to the stable. He helped Mary down. Then he made a soft bed of straw for her on the floor and covered it with his cloak. Mary ate some food and then lay down, thankful that she could rest at last.

That night, Mary's baby son was born. She washed him and wrapped him in the clothes she had brought with her. Joseph filled a manger with soft, clean hay to make a bed for the baby and Mary laid him gently in it. She called her new baby Jesus, as the angel had told her to, and he was the Son of God.

Out on the hills near Bethlehem, some shepherds lay around their camp fire, guarding their flocks of sheep during the night. Suddenly, they saw a brilliant light in the dark sky and an angel stood in front of them. They were very scared.

"Don't be frightened," said the angel. "I have wonderful news for you, and for all people. Tonight the Son of God was born in a stable in Bethlehem."

As the shepherds stared at the angel, more angels appeared in the sky, singing praises to God. "Glory to God in the highest and peace on earth to all people who love him," they sang. Then the light faded and the angels were gone. The night was dark again.

The shepherds were very excited. "We must go to Bethlehem and look for this child," said one shepherd. The others agreed. They gathered up their things and ran as quickly as they could down the dark hills to the little town.

They soon found the stable and, knocking on the door, crept

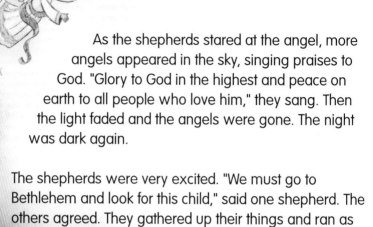

quietly in. They
looked at the baby
lying in the manger
and knelt down in front of him.
They told Mary and Joseph what the
angel had said to them.

After a while, the shepherds got up and left
the stable. They strode through the streets of
Bethlehem, telling everyone they met the good
news that the Son of God had been born that
night. Soon the whole town knew about the
birth of Jesus.

Singing praises to God, the shepherds
walked very happily back to their
sheep on the dark hills outside
Bethlehem.

In the quiet stable, Mary looked at her baby son and thought about the shepherds and what the angel had told them. She wondered what it all meant.

The Wise Men

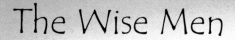

In a country far from Bethlehem lived some Wise Men who studied the stars. One night they saw a new star which was much brighter than all the rest. They knew it must mean something special had happened. After a lot of study, they decided that it meant a new ruler had been born and that they must go to find him.

They began their long journey, taking presents for this new ruler. They followed the star which moved across the night sky ahead of them. At last they arrived in the great city of Jerusalem.

"Tell us where we can find this baby," they said. "We have seen his star in the sky and know he is born to be the King of the Jews."

When King Herod heard that three strangers were trying to find the baby, he was angry and frightened. The Roman rulers of the country had made Herod the King of the Jews. He asked his priests and wise men what it meant. They studied the old records, and told King Herod that, many years ago, it had been forecast that the King of the Jews would be born in Bethlehem.

Herod asked for a secret meeting with the Wise Men. When they came, he told them to go to Bethlehem. "When you find this child, let me know so that I can worship him too," he said. The Wise Men agreed and started at once along the road to Bethlehem. The star still moved ahead of them and then seemed to stop over the town. The Wise Men knew that they'd come to the right place.

They soon found out where Mary and Joseph were. When they saw baby Jesus, the Wise Men knelt down in front of him and gave Mary the presents they had brought with them. The presents were gold, and sweet-smelling frankincense, and a special ointment called myrrh. Then the Wise Men went quietly away.

On their way back to King Herod in Jerusalem, they camped outside Bethlehem. That night, they had a dream. In it, an angel warned them that King Herod planned to kill Jesus. In the morning, they loaded their camels and went, not to Jerusalem, but by a different road back to their own country.

Joseph also had a dream. An angel warned him that Jesus was in danger and he must take Mary and the

baby to Egypt where they would be safe. Joseph woke Mary, and quickly packed up their things. Carrying baby Jesus, they started on their long journey to Egypt while it was still dark.

When King Herod realized he'd been tricked by the Wise Men, he was furious. He was afraid that this new King of the Jews would seize his throne. He ordered his soldiers to march to Bethlehem and kill all the boys under two years old. The people had always hated this cruel king and now they hated him even more.

Mary and Joseph lived safely with Jesus in Egypt. Then Joseph had another dream. An angel told him that King Herod was dead and he should take Mary and Jesus back to Nazareth. After another very long journey, they settled down in their own home.

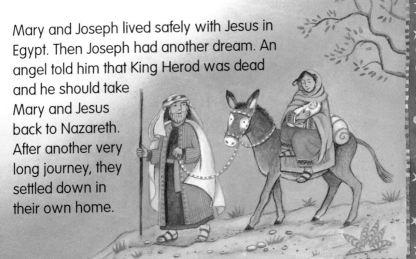

Jesus in the Temple

Jesus grew up in Nazareth, cared for by Mary and Joseph. He went to school and learned the laws God had given to the Jews. Every year, Mary and Joseph went to Jerusalem to celebrate the Feast of the Passover. This festival reminded them that God had freed his people from slavery in Egypt all those years ago.

When Jesus was twelve years old, he went to Jerusalem with his parents. The journey took four days and when they arrived the great city was crowded with visitors.

When the festival was over, Mary and Joseph joined the other families going back to Nazareth. They thought Jesus was in the crowd with the other boys. It wasn't until they stopped in the evening to camp for the night and have a meal that they realized that Jesus was missing. They looked everywhere for him and asked everyone if they had seen him, but they couldn't find him.

Very worried, Mary and Joseph hurried back to Jerusalem. For three days, they searched the city for Jesus. At last, they found him in the Temple. He was sitting with the Temple teachers, listening to them and asking questions. The teachers were amazed that Jesus, who was only twelve, understood so much of what they told him, and were astonished by the questions he asked. Mary and Joseph were very surprised to find him there.

"Why did you do this to us?" Mary asked Jesus. "We've been searching everywhere for you. We were so worried about you. We thought we'd never find you."

"I'm sorry I have caused so much trouble," said Jesus. "But didn't you know you would find me in my Father's house?"

Mary and Joseph didn't understand what Jesus meant. They took him home to Nazareth where he grew up into a wise and strong young man who loved and obeyed his parents and God.

Jesus is Baptized

Jesus stayed in Nazareth with Mary and Joseph until he was about thirty years old. Then he went to Galilee where John, a cousin of his, was telling the people about God and how they should do what He says. Crowds of people came to hear him. When they asked John what they should do, he told them to share their food with hungry people and give their spare clothes to those who needed them.

John baptized the people who were sorry for the bad things they had done. He used water in the Jordan river. This meant they were sorry for their bad lives and could start again by leading good lives.

"I baptize you with water," John told them, "but one is coming who is much greater than I. I'm not worthy to undo his sandals. He will baptize you with the Holy Spirit."

Jesus went to John and asked John to baptize him. But John said, "It's not right for me to baptize you. You should baptize me."

"Let us do what God wants," said Jesus and, saying a prayer, he walked into the river. John poured water over Jesus to show that he had been washed clean. Then, just as Jesus stepped out of the river, Heaven opened and a white dove hovered over his head. And he heard the voice of God say to him, "You are my dear Son. I am very pleased with you."

Jesus and his Disciples

*J*esus lived in Capernaum, a town near Lake Galilee. There he talked to people about God, and healed the ones who were ill. News of his teaching spread quickly and, everywhere he went, crowds of people came to listen to him.

One day, Jesus was walking along the shore of the lake. As usual, people crowded around him. There was a boat pulled up on the shore, owned by a fisherman called Peter and his brother Andrew. Jesus stepped into it. "Row a little way out on the lake so I can speak to the people," said Jesus. The two men did as Jesus asked.

Later, Jesus told Peter and Andrew to row farther away from the shore and put out their fishing nets. "We have fished all night and caught nothing," said Peter. But they did as Jesus told them. When they began to pull in the nets, they were so full of fish, the nets were almost breaking. Peter and Andrew shouted across to two other fishermen, James and John, to come to help. Together, they filled both boats with fish.

When the four men
saw how many fish
they'd caught, they were
very frightened and knelt in front
of Jesus. "Don't be afraid," said Jesus.
"Come with me and I will make you fishermen of people."

Peter and Andrew, James and John rowed back to the
shore and unloaded the fish. Then they left their boats and
went with Jesus on his journeys.

One day, Jesus saw a rich man called Matthew. He
worked for the Romans, collecting taxes. The Jewish
people hated the Romans who ruled them, and hated their
tax collectors even more. Jesus said to Matthew, "Come
with me." Without saying a word, Matthew stood up and
followed Jesus and the other disciples.

Matthew gave a feast in his house for Jesus. Some religious people saw Jesus there. They asked Jesus' friends why such a good man sat down at a table with so many bad people. Jesus heard them. "Healthy people don't need a doctor," he said. "It's the sick who need help. I have come to ask the bad people to change their ways. The good people don't need me."

One evening Jesus walked high up a mountain and stayed there all night, praying to God. The next day, he chose the rest of his disciples. They were Philip and Bartholomew, Thomas, another James, Simon, Judas and Judas Iscariot. With Peter, Andrew, James, John and Matthew, these twelve men were Jesus' special friends and followers. They went everywhere with him, listened to his teachings and watched the wonderful things he did. He told them what God had sent him to do.

Jesus and the Paralysed Man

News that Jesus was teaching people about God and making those who were ill well again spread very quickly. Wherever he went with his twelve disciples, crowds of people came from all over the country, and from the city of Jerusalem, to listen to him and to be healed of all kinds of diseases.

One day, Jesus was sitting in a house that was so packed with people, there was no room for anyone to move in or out. Four friends of a very ill man carried him on a stretcher to the house. The man was paralysed and couldn't move at all.

When the four friends saw they couldn't get into the house by the door, they lifted the stretcher up to the flat roof. Then they made a hole in the roof and lowered the stretcher and the sick man down into the room where Jesus was sitting.

Jesus looked at the four friends and saw the faith they had in him. Then he said to the sick man, "My son," he said, "your sins are forgiven."

The Jewish leaders who heard Jesus say this whispered angrily to each other. Jesus had no right to forgive sins, they said; only God could do that.

Jesus knew what they were saying. "Is it easier," he asked them, "to forgive a man for the bad things he has done or to make him walk again? To show you that I have the power to forgive sins. . ." Jesus stopped and turned to the man on the stretcher. "Get up, pick up your stretcher and go home," he said.

Without saying a word, the man at once stood up and, taking the stretcher with him, walked out of the house. He went home, saying a prayer of thanks to God.

The people in the house were very excited and a little frightened. They talked to each other and praised God. They had never seen anything like this before.

The Sermon on the Mountain

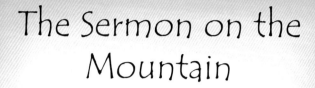

Wherever Jesus went with his disciples, crowds of people came to listen to him. On the Sabbath, he taught them in the synagogues, but most of the time he talked to them out of doors, as the weather was often hot and dry.

One day, he walked up a mountain. The people sat down so they could see and hear him. Jesus told them that those people who were really hungry to know God would be satisfied. He told them they should be content and not worry about food or clothing. "Look at the birds," he said. "They don't grow and store food but God takes care of them and He will take care of you. Look at the beautiful flowers. They don't make their clothes. Even the great King Solomon wasn't better dressed than them. Don't worry about what might happen. Do what God wants you to do and he will give you what you need."

"It's easy to love your friends, but you should love all people and be kind to those who are nasty to you. When you do someone a good turn, do it secretly and don't tell everybody about it. God will see you and reward you."

"When you say a prayer to God, do it quietly when you are on your own. Talk to God as you would to a father who loves you. Don't ask for the same thing over and over again. God knows what you need."

"Say this prayer when you speak to God:
    Our Father who is in Heaven
    Holy is your name,
    May your Kingdom come,
    May your will be done on earth as it is in Heaven.
    Give us our food each day,
    Forgive us the wrongs we have done,
    As we forgive the wrongs others have done to us.
    Do not let us be tempted to do wrong.
    But save us from evil."

"Anyone who listens to me," said Jesus, "and does what I say is like a man who builds a house on solid rock. When it rains and the wind blows and the floods come, his house will stand strong and firm. But anyone who hears me and does not do what I say is like a man who builds his house on the sand. When it rains, the wind blows and the floods come, his house will be washed away because it was built only on soft sand."

27

Jesus Calms the Storm

One evening, when Jesus was tired after talking to people all day and making the sick ones well again, he asked some of his disciples to take him across Lake Galilee. There was just a gentle breeze blowing when they pushed the boat down the beach and floated it on the lake. The disciples hoisted the sail and the boat skimmed away across the smooth water.

Jesus lay down in the
bottom of the boat and was
soon fast asleep.

Suddenly the wind started blowing
stronger and stronger until there was a
great storm. The waves grew bigger and bigger
and splashed over the side of the boat. The
disciples were very scared. Some of them were
fishermen and knew how dangerous storms on the
lake could be. They thought the boat would fill with
water and sink. Although the wind was so noisy and the
waves so rough, Jesus just slept on.

At last, one of the disciples could bear it no longer. He shook Jesus and woke him up.

"Master, please save us," he shouted. "Can't you see that we're all going to drown?"

Jesus woke up and looked at the storm for a moment. Then he stood up, raised his arm and said, "Hush, be still." At once, the wind died away and the waves became calm.

"Why were you afraid?" Jesus asked the disciples. "Don't you believe I will take care of you?"

The disciples didn't know what to say. They whispered to each other. "Who is this man that even the wind and the waves do as he tells them?"

The boat sailed on and Jesus and his disciples safely reached the far shore of the lake.

The Good Shepherd

*J*esus often told people stories so that they could understand more easily what he was trying to teach them. The stories were about the things they saw every day and some of the work they did. He said to the men, women and children who came to hear him, "If you have ears, listen to what I say."

One day, he began a new story. "If a shepherd has a hundred sheep to look after and one of them wanders off and gets lost, what does the shepherd do?" he asked the people. "He leaves the ninety-nine sheep," Jesus went on, "where he knows they are safe from hungry wolves and goes off in search of the one missing sheep."

"The shepherd searches everywhere for that one sheep, listening all the time to hear it bleating. However long it takes, he doesn't give up until he finds it. Then he picks up the sheep, puts it on his shoulders and carries it home, delighted that it is safely back with the rest of the flock."

"Then he calls his family and friends to come and celebrate with him that he has found his one lost sheep."

"There is joy in Heaven," said Jesus, "when someone who has disobeyed God is sorry for the bad things he or she has done and comes back to do as God wants them to do."

"I am like that good shepherd. I look after my people as if they were my sheep. I never run away and leave them when wolves try to kill them. The sheep know my voice and follow me. I lead them and protect them. I am ready to die for them," said Jesus.

Jairus's Daughter

When Jesus was walking through a town one day, a ruler of the synagogue, called Jairus, ran up to him. He knelt in front of Jesus. "My little daughter is very ill; I think she is dying. Please come to my house and put your hands on her so she may get better," he begged.

As Jesus started to go with Jairus, a woman pushed through the crowd following them to get near to Jesus. She had been ill for twelve years and none of the doctors had been able to help her; she only got worse.

She had heard of Jesus. She thought, "If I could only touch his clothes, I know I will be well at last." When she was close, she put out her hand and touched him. At once, she was completely cured. Jesus looked at the people crowding around him. "Who touched me?" he asked, knowing that someone had been healed.

The woman was very frightened. She knelt in front of Jesus and told him she had touched him. Jesus looked

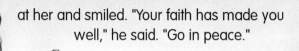

at her and smiled. "Your faith has made you well," he said. "Go in peace."

Jesus walked on to Jairus's house but, before he got there, people came out weeping. "It is too late," they cried to Jairus. "Your little daughter is dead. Don't ask Jesus to come."

"She is not dead. She is asleep," said Jesus, and he went on to the house, with three disciples, Peter, James and John. Jesus made everyone leave the house, except the mother and father of the little girl. Then he gently held the girl's hand and said, "Little girl, get up."

At once, the girl opened her eyes and got up off her bed. The girl's mother and father were astonished and thrilled to see their daughter alive and well. "Now give her something to eat," said Jesus, "but don't tell anyone about this." And he and his three disciples walked quietly out of the house.

Loaves and Fishes

One day, Jesus was feeling tired and wanted to go to a quiet place to have a little time by himself. He and his disciples sailed across Lake Galilee to a lonely beach. They landed on the shore, pulled up the boat and walked up a hill to rest. But some people had seen where Jesus went and news that he was there quickly spread. Soon people started to walk from the towns and villages to see and hear him.

The disciples wanted to send the people away but Jesus felt sorry for them. He walked among them, talking to them, answering their questions and making the ill ones well. More and more people came until there were thousands of them.

In the evening, a disciple said to Jesus, "It's time these people went home. Send them away now so they can find food. There's nothing here for them to eat."

Jesus said, "They are hungry, we must feed them first."

"There is nowhere to buy food, and even a huge amount of money wouldn't buy enough to feed all these people," said Philip, one of the disciples.

Andrew, another disciple, said to Jesus, "There is a boy here who has five small loaves and two fishes."

Jesus looked down at the boy. "May I take your food?" Jesus asked him. "Yes, Master," said the boy.

"Tell the people to sit down in groups," Jesus said to the disciples. The disciples walked through the crowd asking everyone to sit down on the grass. There were about five thousand men, women and children.

Jesus held up the boy's five small loaves and two little fishes, and said a prayer to God. Then he broke up the bread and fishes and handed them to the disciples to give to the people. The more food the disciples gave out, the more there was. They were very surprised and very puzzled.

Everybody began to eat and they all had as much as they wanted. When the meal was over, the people got up and went home in the late evening.

"Collect all the leftover food," Jesus said to the disciples. They walked over the hillside, picking up the food. When they'd finished, they'd filled twelve baskets with bits of bread and fish.

The Good Samaritan

When Jesus was teaching the people about God, a clever lawyer stood up and asked him, "I know I should be kind to other people, but who does that mean?"

Jesus told him this story. "A Jew who lived in Jerusalem left the city and began the long walk to Jericho. Although the Jew knew it was dangerous to travel alone, because there were robbers on the road, he went on his own."

"When the Jew came to a lonely spot, some robbers rushed out and attacked him. They beat him, knocked him down and kicked him. Then they stole all he had and ran away, leaving him lying on the ground, badly wounded."

"After a while, a priest from the Temple came down the road. He saw the Jew lying in the dust, but dug his heels into his donkey and hurried away."

"Later, a man who worked in the Temple in Jerusalem came up. He looked at the wounded Jew for a moment but didn't stop. He went on quickly away down the road."

"Then a Samaritan trotted up on his donkey. The Samaritans and the Jews had always hated each other. But this Samaritan felt sorry for the Jew. He stopped and got off his donkey. He opened his pack and, kneeling by the man, poured oil on his wounds to ease the pain and gave him wine to drink to make him feel better. Then he bandaged the man with strips of cloth."

"When the Samaritan had done all he could, he lifted the Jew up on his donkey and led it down the road to an inn. There he put the Jew to bed and bought him supper."

"The next morning, the Samaritan paid the innkeeper. 'Look after this man for me,' he said. 'I will pay you any extra money I owe you when I come this way again.'"

"Now," Jesus asked the lawyer, "which of the three men was kind?"

"The Samaritan, of course," replied the lawyer. "That is the answer to your question," said Jesus. "You should be kind to everyone, not just your family and friends, but everyone."

Mary, Martha and Lazarus

When Jesus visited a village called Bethany, near Jerusalem, he stayed with two sisters, Mary and Martha, and their brother Lazarus.

One day, Mary and Martha sent a message to Jesus, telling him that Lazarus was very ill and asking him to come and save their brother's life. They expected Jesus to come at once, but they waited for two days and Jesus still had not come.

"Our friend Lazarus is sleeping. I'll go and wake him up," Jesus said to his twelve disciples. "Won't sleep make him better?" asked the disciples. But Jesus knew that Lazarus was dead.

When Jesus and his disciples reached Bethany at last, Lazarus had been in his tomb for four days. Mary stayed in the house with her weeping friends but Martha ran out to meet Jesus. "Lord, if you had been here, my brother would not have died," she cried.

"He will live again," said Jesus.

"I know he will when God brings all the dead back to life on the last day," said Martha. "Everyone who trusts in me will live for ever, even if they die," Jesus said to her.

Then Mary came out of the house, crying, with the friends and relations who had come to comfort her. Jesus felt very sorry for her and was sad. "Take me to Lazarus," he said. They led him to the tomb which was a cave. In front of it was a big rock. "Move the rock away," said Jesus.

"But Lazarus has been dead for four days. He will smell bad," said Martha. "I told you that if you would trust me, you shall see God's glory," Jesus told her.

Friends of the two sisters rolled away the rock in front of the tomb. Jesus said a prayer to God and then shouted, "Lazarus, come out."

Lazarus walked out of the tomb, wearing the clothes he had been buried in, but alive and well.

41

The Prodigal Son

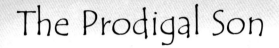

Jesus was talking to a crowd of people when some of the religious people muttered, "Why does this man talk and eat with bad people?" Jesus heard them and told them, "When only one bad person is sorry for what he has done and wants to please God, there is joy in Heaven." And he told them this story.

"A rich farmer had two sons. One day, the younger son said, 'Father, one day half of everything you have will be mine. Give it to me now.' The father was very unhappy but he did as

his son demanded and gave him a lot of his money."

"A few days later, the son rode away to a city, taking the money with him. He bought rich clothes and a big house with lots of servants, and soon made many new friends. Every evening, he gave great feasts for his friends, with delicious food and good wine."

"He thought he was having a wonderful time. But soon he had spent all his money. His new friends left him, his house and servants were taken away from him, and he had nothing left, not even his fine clothes."

"He wandered the streets, begging for something to eat. But as there was a shortage of food in the city, no one had any to spare, and he had to go hungry."

"At last he got a job looking after a man's pigs in the fields. Sometimes he was so hungry, he was tempted to eat the pigs' food. One day, as he was watching the pigs, he thought, 'My father's servants always have plenty to eat, while I'm nearly dying of hunger. I'll go home and beg my father to forgive me.'"

"After a long journey, the son reached his home, tired, dirty and wearing rags. When he was still some way from the house, his father saw him. He felt very sorry for his son and ran to meet him. He threw his arms around him and hugged him."

"'Forgive me, father. I've been very foolish,' said the son. 'I don't deserve to be your son any more. Let me be one of your servants.'"

"The father took his son home. He told his servants to bring new clothes and shoes for his son. He was so happy, he ordered a special dinner that night and told everyone they should join in the party."

"Out in the fields, the elder son heard the noise of laughter and music. He walked back to the house and asked one of the servants what it was all about."

"'Your brother has come home and your father is giving him a special dinner, with music and dancing, because he is so pleased to see his son again,' said the servant."

"The elder son was very angry and refused to go into the house. His father went out and asked him to come in."

"'I've worked hard for you all these years but you've never given me anything. You've never given a party for me and my friends,' shouted the son. 'But as soon as your other son comes home, having wasted half your money, you order a great feast for him.'"

"'My son,' said the father, 'you are always with me and everything I have is yours. Please try to understand. I thought your brother was lost or dead. I'm so happy he has come home again, alive and well.'"

Jesus Rides into Jerusalem

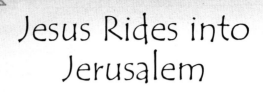

Jesus and his twelve disciples walked to the great city of Jerusalem to be there in time for the special festival of the Passover. On the way, they stopped near a small village called Bethany.

Jesus said to two of his disciples, "Go into the village. There you will find a donkey that has never been ridden. Untie it and

bring it here. If anyone asks you why you are taking it, tell him, 'The Lord needs it,' and he will let you have it."

The two disciples did as Jesus told them and soon came back with the donkey. They spread their cloaks over it to make a soft saddle and Jesus got on the donkey. Then he rode into Jerusalem with his disciples walking at his side.

When the crowds of people walking to the city saw Jesus coming, they were excited. Some spread their cloaks on the road. Others cut down palm leaves to lay in front of him. They cheered and shouted, "Blessed is he who comes in the name of the Lord. Praise be to God."

Jesus and his disciples went into the city and walked through the streets to the Temple. Then they left and went back to the village of Bethany for the night.

The next morning, Jesus went again to the Temple to pray. It was like a crowded market with people buying and selling cows, sheep and doves, and changing money. Jesus was very angry. He stormed through it, overturning the tables and the seats of the sellers and driving them, and the animals and birds out of the Temple.

"God's house is a house of prayer," he shouted, "but you have turned it into a den of robbers."

When all was quiet and peaceful again, he talked to the

crowds of people, teaching them about God and making the ill ones well again.

The Temple rulers heard what Jesus had done and decided they must get rid of him. They didn't dare arrest him in the Temple because they were afraid the people would riot to protect him. They plotted to do it secretly.

Then Judas Iscariot, one of Jesus' disciples, went secretly to the chief priests of the Temple. "What will you give me if I tell you when it would be safe to arrest Jesus?" he asked. They promised to give him thirty silver coins. From then on, Judas Iscariot waited and watched for the right moment to give Jesus away to the Temple priests. It had to be when there were no crowds around to see the arrest.

The Last Supper

A few days before the Feast
of the Passover, which reminded the Jews of when God
freed them from being slaves in Egypt, Jesus' disciples
asked him where they should have the special meal.

"Go to Jerusalem," said Jesus to Peter and John. "There
you will meet a man carrying a jar of water. Follow him to
his house. We will have our meal there in a room
upstairs."

The two men went to Jerusalem and found the house.
They made the room ready and that evening Jesus and
the other ten disciples came upstairs.

Before the meal began, Jesus picked up a towel and a
bowl of water. He knelt in front of each disciple
in turn, and washed their feet and dried
them with a towel, just like a
servant. When he had finished,
he said, "You must be ready to
serve each other in the same

way that I have served you."

Then Jesus sat down again at the table. The disciples watched him quietly. They could see something was wrong. Jesus looked very sad because he knew he wouldn't be with them much longer, but would die soon.

At last, he said, "One of you will betray me." The disciples were horrified. They all looked at each other and wondered who it could be. Then one, who was sitting next to Jesus, asked, "Which one of us is it, Lord?" "It is the one I give this bread to," answered Jesus.

He broke off a piece of bread, dipped it in a dish and handed it to Judas Iscariot. "Do what you have to do," he said. Judas Iscariot got up from the table and slipped quickly out of the room into the night.

Then Jesus picked up a loaf of bread and said a prayer to God. He broke up the bread and passed the pieces to the disciples.

"Eat this bread which is my body and remember me," he said. Then he picked up a cup of wine, said a prayer, and

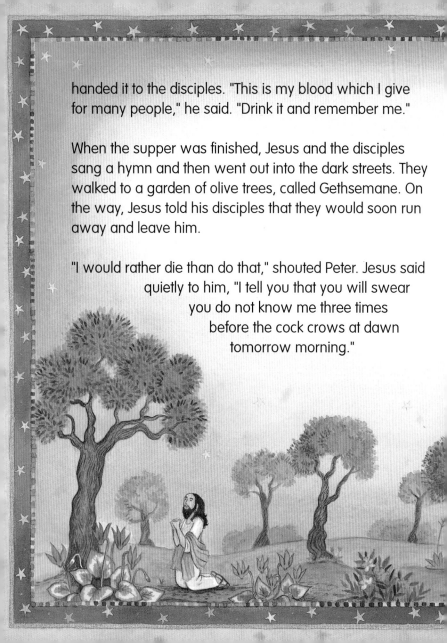

handed it to the disciples. "This is my blood which I give for many people," he said. "Drink it and remember me."

When the supper was finished, Jesus and the disciples sang a hymn and then went out into the dark streets. They walked to a garden of olive trees, called Gethsemane. On the way, Jesus told his disciples that they would soon run away and leave him.

"I would rather die than do that," shouted Peter. Jesus said quietly to him, "I tell you that you will swear you do not know me three times before the cock crows at dawn tomorrow morning."

At Gethsemane, he asked some of the disciples to stay near the gates of the garden while he prayed to God. He walked away to a quiet place with Peter, James and John, and then went on alone to pray for the courage to face the terrible time that was coming.

When he went back to Peter, James and John, Jesus found they were fast asleep. "Couldn't you stay awake for just one hour?" he asked. "Please keep watch while I pray," and he walked away. After he had said his prayers, Jesus again went back to the three disciples and, again, they were asleep.

The third time Jesus woke up the disciples, they could hear loud voices and see torches flaring in the dark. It was the chief priests with the Temple guards. Judas Iscariot was leading them to where they could find and arrest Jesus.

Judas walked up to Jesus and kissed him on the cheek. "This is the man you want," he said to the guards. When the guards closed in, Peter drew his sword and tried to defend Jesus. He slashed off an ear of one of the High Priest's servants.

"Put down your sword," Jesus told Peter and, touching the man's ear, made it whole again.

The disciples were very frightened. They ran away, just as Jesus said they would. They left him alone to be marched by the guards back to Jerusalem.

Death on a Cross

Late that night, Jesus was taken by the Temple guards to the palace of Caiaphas, the High Priest. Many of the Jewish leaders were called there to put Jesus on trial.

Peter secretly followed Jesus through the streets to the palace courtyard. As he stood with some of the guards, warming himself by their fire, a servant girl walked past and looked at him. "You were with Jesus," she said. "I don't know what you mean," said Peter. Then another servant said, "This man was with Jesus." "I don't know him," swore Peter.

Later a man said, "You must know Jesus. I can tell you come from Galilee." Peter was very frightened. "I tell you, I don't know the man," he shouted. Then a cock crowed three times and Peter remembered that Jesus had told him he would deny knowing him.

Peter was so ashamed of himself, he ran out of the courtyard and into a dark corner, where he cried.

In the palace, the chief priests and the Jewish leaders began the trial of Jesus. They brought in many people who told lies about Jesus. But their stories did not match up. The leaders wanted to find an excuse to kill Jesus, but they couldn't prove he'd done anything wrong. All through the trial, Jesus said nothing and wouldn't answer any of the charges.

In the end, the High Priest asked Jesus if he was the Son of God. "I am," answered Jesus, quietly. "You heard what the prisoner said," the High Priest told the people there. "Do you find him guilty or not guilty of a crime against God?" "Guilty," shouted the people, and they hit Jesus and spat at him.

The High Priest sentenced Jesus, but before he could have Jesus put to death, he had to take him to Pontius Pilate, the Roman Governor. Only the Roman Governor could give the order for an execution.

When Judas heard that Jesus was to die, he was terribly

sorry he'd given Jesus away to the chief priests. He went to the Temple and threw down the thirty silver coins they'd given him. Then he went out and hanged himself.

In the morning, Jesus was taken to Pontius Pilate. The chief priests knew the Roman Governor wouldn't sentence a man to death for a crime against God, so they accused him of a crime against the Roman laws.

Jesus stood in front of the Roman Governor, who asked him questions but Jesus didn't reply. In the end, the Governor realized Jesus was innocent but he didn't want to make the Jewish leaders angry by setting him free.

At that time, it was the custom for the Roman rulers of the country to set one prisoner free at the Feast of the Passover. The people could choose who it would be. Pontius Pilate asked the crowd if he should free Barabbas, who was a murderer, or Jesus. The chief priests and Jewish leaders persuaded the crowd to ask for Barabbas.

"What shall I do with Jesus?" Pontius Pilate asked the people. "Crucify him, crucify him," they shouted. "What harm has he done?" asked Pontius. But the people just

shouted again, "Crucify him." Pontius turned away and washed his hands in a bowl of water to show that he was not to blame for Jesus' death.

Then he gave the order that Barabbas should be set free and Jesus was to be whipped before he was put to death. The guards took Jesus away and dressed him in a purple robe, pressed a crown made of thorns on his head and put a stick in his hand. They knelt in front of him, laughing and jeering. "Hail, King of the Jews," they mocked, beating him and spitting at him.

Then the guards dressed Jesus in his own clothes and made him carry a huge wooden cross through the streets of Jerusalem. Tired and weak from the beatings, Jesus stumbled and fell down again and again. At last, a soldier made a man called Simon, who was standing in the street watching, carry the cross for Jesus.

They led Jesus outside the city to a place called Golgotha. There the guards nailed Jesus' hands and feet to the cross.

They put a sign above his head which said, "Jesus of Nazareth. King of the Jews." Then they set up the cross between two other crosses. On them were thieves who had been sentenced to death. Jesus looked down at the soldiers and the people watching. "Forgive them, Father," he prayed. "They do not know what they are doing."

Some of Jesus' enemies were in the crowd. "If you really are the Son of God, come down from the cross. Then we'll believe you," they jeered. And the chief priests called, "You saved others, why don't you save yourself?"

Mary, Jesus' mother, was standing near the cross with John, one of the disciples. Jesus looked down at them. "Take care of her as if you were her son," he said to John. And from then on, John looked after Mary.

At noon, it grew strangely dark for about three hours. The crowd watched and waited in silence. At three o'clock, Jesus looked up and cried, "My God, why have you forgotten me?" Bowing his head, he said, "It is finished," and died. At that moment, the ground shook and the curtain in the Temple ripped from top to bottom. Many of the soldiers and the people were very frightened.

A Roman soldier looked up at Jesus. "This man really was the Son of God," he said.

The crowds drifted away to the city but Mary, Jesus' mother, Mary Magdalene, and the mother of James, and some of Jesus' other friends stayed by the cross. To make sure Jesus was dead, a soldier thrust a spear into his side. Then the soldiers took Jesus down from the cross.

A rich man from Arimathea, called Joseph, who believed in Jesus, went to the Roman Governor, Pontius Pilate. He asked to be allowed to take Jesus away for burial. Pilate agreed and ordered that Joseph should be given the body.

With some of Jesus' other friends, Joseph carried the body away and wrapped it in a linen cloth. Then they took it to a new tomb which had been cut into the rock on a hillside garden outside Jerusalem. Watched by Mary Magdalene and some other women, they laid the

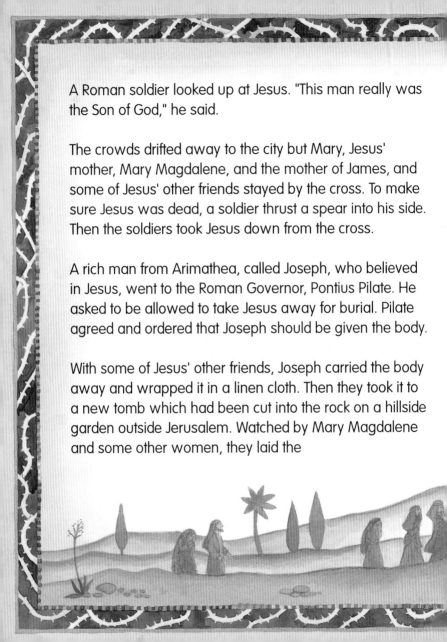

body in the tomb. Then they rolled a heavy stone in front of it, like a door, to close it. It was now Friday evening. The Jewish Sabbath begins at sunset and Jesus' friends had to leave the proper burial of Jesus until the Sabbath on Saturday was over.

The Jewish leaders asked Pontius Pilate to put a guard on the tomb. They were afraid someone might try to steal the body and claim that Jesus had come alive again. Pilate gave the order. His soldiers put a seal on the tomb and stood guard over it during the night.

The Empty Tomb

Very early on Sunday morning, Mary Magdalene and two women friends went to Jesus' tomb. They wanted to finish the preparations for the burial. They wondered how they would roll away the huge stone that blocked the entrance.

When the women reached the tomb, they were surprised to see that the stone had been rolled away and the soldiers guarding it had gone. A man in shining white clothes told them, "Jesus is not here. He is alive." When they looked into the tomb, they saw it was empty. The body was gone.

Puzzled and frightened, the three women ran to tell two

disciples, Peter and John. "They've taken the Lord away," cried Mary, "and we don't know where they've laid him."

Peter and John ran to the tomb. John got there first, but didn't want to go in. When Peter came, he went straight in and saw the tomb was empty. But the cloths Jesus had been wrapped in were there. Peter and John didn't know if the body had been stolen or if Jesus had really come alive again. Very puzzled, they went quietly home.

Mary Magdalene went back to the tomb on her own. While she knelt, crying, outside the tomb, Jesus came and stood beside her. "Why are you crying?" he asked. "Who are you looking for?" Mary didn't look up. She thought it must be a gardener. "I'm crying because they have taken my Lord away. Please tell me where he is," she begged.

"Mary," said Jesus. Mary looked up and saw it was Jesus. "My Master," she cried. "Go and tell my friends you have seen me," said Jesus, "and that soon I will be with my Father in Heaven." Full of joy, Mary ran to tell the disciples that she had seen Jesus and that he had spoken to her.

On the Road to Emmaus

Later, on that Sunday evening, two of Jesus' friends were walking along the road from Jerusalem to the village of Emmaus. As they walked, they talked about Jesus.

Soon Jesus caught up with them and walked along with them. But they didn't recognize him and thought he was a stranger. "Why are you so sad?" he asked them.

"Are you the only stranger in all of Jerusalem who doesn't know what has happened there over the last few days?" asked one of the men, whose name was Cleopas.

"Why, what has happened?" asked the stranger.

"We are talking about Jesus of Nazareth," said the other man. "He was a great teacher. We believed he was sent by God to save our people. But the chief priests and our

Roman rulers said he broke the laws and must die. They nailed him to a cross last Friday and now he is dead. When some women went to his tomb today, they found that his body had gone. They said angels told them that Jesus is alive."

The stranger told them that the prophets had said all this would happen and explained it to them. At last, they reached Emmaus late in the evening. The stranger looked as if he would walk on, but the two men invited him to stay and have supper with them.

When they sat down to eat, the stranger picked up a loaf of bread, said a prayer, broke the bread into pieces and gave it to the two men. Then the two men knew that the stranger was Jesus. They stared at him for a moment and then he was gone.

Very excited, the two men got up from the table and ran all the way back to Jerusalem. They soon found the disciples and some of Jesus' other friends. They told them that they had seen Jesus, had spoken to him and that he was alive. At first, the disciples did not believe them but one said, "It must be true; Peter has seen him."

They locked the door of the room because they were afraid of the Roman rulers and chief priests. Then, suddenly, Jesus was in the room with them. At first, they were scared. They thought that he must be a ghost.

Jesus said, "Don't be afraid. Look at the wounds on my hands and feet. Touch me and see that I am made of flesh and bone." Then they knew that he really was Jesus.

"Have you anything to eat?" asked Jesus. They gave him some cooked fish and some honey comb and watched him eat it. At last, they were convinced that Jesus really was alive. He explained to them that this was all part of God's plan and that it had all been foretold by the prophets.

"Christ had to die and to come alive again on the third day," he said. "God forgives everyone who believes in Him. This is the message for all the people in the world and you must go and tell them."

Thomas, the doubter

Thomas, one of the disciples, was not with the others when they saw Jesus. He wouldn't believe it when they told him Jesus was alive. "I won't believe it until I see the marks of the nails on his hands and feet, and touch the wound in his side," he said.

A week later, Thomas was with the other disciples and the door of the room was locked. Suddenly, Jesus was with them again.

"Thomas," he said, "put your finger on the marks on my hands and on the wound in my side. Stop doubting and believe what you see."

Thomas didn't touch Jesus. He did not need to. "My Lord and my God," he said. "You now believe because you have seen me with your own eyes," said Jesus. "But more trusting are the people who have not seen me but still believe in me."

Breakfast by the Lake

During the next few weeks, Jesus' disciples and friends often saw him. One evening, Peter and some other disciples left Jerusalem and went to Lake Galilee. Peter said he wanted to go fishing. With the others, he stepped aboard a boat and they set sail across the lake. They fished all night but caught nothing. In the morning, when they were sailing back to the shore, they saw a man standing beside the lake. They didn't know it was Jesus.

"Have you caught any fish?" he called to them. "No, nothing," they shouted back.

"Throw your net over the right side of the ship," called Jesus. They did as he said and the net was soon so full of fish, they couldn't pull it in.

One of the disciples said, "It must be Jesus." Peter immediately jumped overboard and swam to the shore. The other men rowed the boat to the beach, dragging in the net bulging with fish. Jesus had lit a fire and he cooked some of the fish over it.

"Come and eat," said Jesus and gave them the cooked fish and some bread. No one dared asked him who he was but they all knew it was Jesus.

When they had finished eating, Jesus asked Peter, "Do you love me?" "You know I do," said Peter. Jesus asked Peter the same question two more times and each time Peter said he did love him. And each time, Jesus told him to take good care of his followers.

Wind and Fire

The last time his disciples saw Jesus was when they were walking on the Mount of Olives outside Jerusalem. He came to say goodbye.

"You must go back to Jerusalem," Jesus told them. "Wait there and soon God will send you the Holy Spirit. He will give you the power to speak bravely about me and all that I have taught you. You will speak to the people in Jerusalem and in many parts of the country, and even the whole world. Remember, I shall always be with you."

As the disciples watched, a cloud hid Jesus and he was taken up into Heaven. They looked up and saw two men dressed in white. "Jesus has gone to be with God but one day he will come back," they said.

The disciples went back to Jerusalem, feeling very happy, and waited as Jesus had told them. On the day of the Jewish festival of Pentecost, many of Jesus' friends, his mother Mary and some other women were with the disciples in a house in Jerusalem.

Suddenly, they heard noise like a great wind blowing through the room, but the air was still. Then fiery flames flickered around their heads but didn't burn them.

They knew this was the sign that God had sent his power to them. Now they could speak bravely to all people. The disciples rushed out into the streets of Jerusalem and told everyone they met about Jesus and the wonderful things he had done. They spoke in many different languages they had never learned so that everyone could understand them. The disciples told the people that they should be

baptized in the name of Jesus. They should be sorry for the bad things they had done, believe that Jesus died for them, and that God would always help them and be with them.

First published in 2007 by Usborne Publishing Ltd,
83-85 Saffron Hill, London EC1N 8RT, England.
www.usborne.com. Copyright © 2007, 2000, 1998 Usborne
Publishing Ltd. The name Usborne and the devices
are Trade Marks of Usborne Publishing Ltd. All rights reserved.
No part of this publication may be reproduced, stored in a
retrieval system, or transmitted in any form or by any
means, electronic, mechanical, photocopying,
recording or otherwise, without the prior
permission of the publisher. First published
in America in November 1998.
Printed in Dubai.